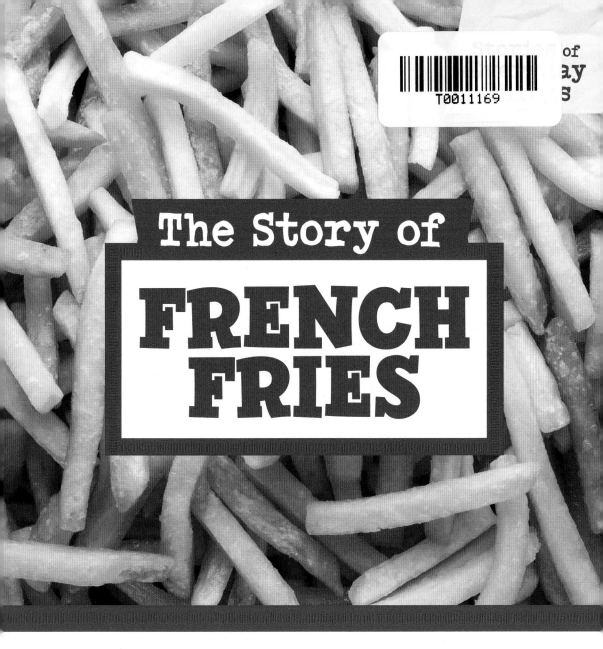

The Story of
FRENCH FRIES

by Gloria Koster

PEBBLE
a capstone imprint

Published by Pebble, an imprint of Capstone
1710 Roe Crest Drive, North Mankato, Minnesota 56003
capstonepub.com

Library of Congress Cataloging-in-Publication Data
Names: Koster, Gloria, author.
Title: The story of french fries / by Gloria Koster.
Description: North Mankato, Minnesota : Pebble, an imprint of
Capstone, [2024] | Series: Stories of everyday things | Includes
bibliographical references and index. | Audience: Ages 5-8
Audience: Grades 2-3
Summary: "Potatoes can be turned into lots of yummy side dishes,
and french fries are a popular option. But who discovered french
fries? Are they really from France? And how did they end up in
restaurants around the world? These questions and more will be
answered in this fascinating book on french fries."—Provided by
publisher.
Identifiers: LCCN 2023027890 (print) | LCCN 2023027891 (ebook)
| ISBN 9780756577490 (hardcover) | ISBN 9780756577810
(paperback) | ISBN 9780756577551 (pdf) | ISBN 9780756577834
(kindle edition) | ISBN 9780756577827 (epub)
Subjects: LCSH: French fries—Juvenile literature. | Cooking
(Potatoes)—Juvenile literature.
Classification: LCC TX803.P8 K64 2024 (print) | LCC TX803.P8
(ebook) |
DDC 641.6/521—dc23/eng/20230623
LC record available at https://lccn.loc.gov/2023027890
LC ebook record available at https://lccn.loc.gov/2023027891

Editorial Credits
Editor: Alison Deering; Designer: Jaime Willems; Media Researcher:
Rebekah Hubstenberger; Production Specialist: Whitney Schaefer

Image Credits
Getty Images: DAJ, 23, Elizabeth Fernandez, 12, elzauer, 22, iStock/
Alex Lupu, 21, iStock/Sonja Rachbauer, 10, Jose Luis Pelaez Inc,
7, Kean Collection, 14, MARTIN BUREAU/AFP, 20, NickyLloyd,
19, Photo by Roo Lewis, 26, SolStock, Back Cover, 5, Stefan
Tomic, 15, Three Lions, 13, Tim Boyle, 24; Shutterstock: Africa
Studio, 1, Alissala, 25, DenisMArt, Cover (bottom right), EQRoy, 9,
Joshua Resnick, 27, New Africa, 18, Olga Bondas, 17, P Maxwell
Photography, Cover, Robert Biedermann, 11, stockcreations, Cover, 6

Design Elements
Shutterstock: Luria, Pooretat moonsana

All internet sites appearing in back matter were available
and accurate when this book was sent to press.

Printed and bound in China. PO 5593

Table of Contents

Words in bold appear in the glossary.

A Tasty Treat

A family orders lunch at a fast-food restaurant. "Would you like fries with that?" the server asks.

"Yes," says the mom. "That's our favorite part of the meal!"

A girl helps her dad make dinner. They are having hamburgers. But there are no fries in their freezer.

"Let's make our own," says the dad. "We have potatoes and oil. That's all we need."

French fries come in different shapes and sizes. There are more than 15 different kinds of fries! They can be thick or thin. They can be curly, waffle cut, or crinkle cut.

No matter how you slice them, people around the world love french fries. Americans eat more than 4 billion pounds each year. They even have a holiday for this special food. National French Fry Day is celebrated each July!

The First French Fries

Where did french fries come from? It depends on who you ask. France, Belgium, and Spain all claim credit for this tasty treat.

Belgians claim to have created fries in the 1600s. One story says that locals used to eat fried fish. But one winter, the river froze. People had to find something else to eat. They chopped and fried potatoes instead.

French fries are the national dish of Belgium. In that country, they are called frites. That's French for fries. Many towns have french fry stands. One city even has a french fry museum!

The Friet Museum is the only museum dedicated to fries.

People in France were not always potato fans. They thought potatoes made people sick. They only fed them to pigs. In 1748, it became illegal to grow or eat potatoes.

potato flowers

Then a doctor changed people's minds. He said potatoes were good for them. They became very popular. Queen Marie Antoinette wore potato flowers in her hair. People cooked potatoes at home. They sold frites on city streets.

In the 1500s, Spanish explorers went to South America. They discovered a vegetable they had not seen before. It was the potato. They brought potatoes back to Spain. There, fries are called papas fritas.

A man fries potato rings in Madrid, Spain.

Frying food in oil is part of Spanish cooking. It is likely that they prepared potatoes that way.

Spain also used to rule Belgium. It's possible fries started there and spread to Belgium.

Thomas Jefferson

Before he was elected president of the United States, Thomas Jefferson spent five years in France. He brought his favorite recipes back to the U.S. That included fried potatoes. He even served them at the **White House**.

During World War I (1914-1918), American soldiers fought in France and Belgium. They tasted fried potatoes. Back home, they gave the dish an English name. Frites became french fries.

The word *french* can also mean to cut something in strips. That is how potatoes are turned into fries. So the name may have nothing to do with a country at all!

A potato is frenched.

From Potato to French Fry

Farmers grow many types of potatoes. They can be white, yellow, or red. Potatoes can even be blue or purple. This vegetable can grow almost anywhere.

Potatoes are made up of **starch** and water. They are covered in a thin skin. This contains **nutrients**. Potatoes also have eyes. These small bumps appear when potatoes start to sprout.

Making french fries is easy. First potatoes are washed. Often skins are peeled. Then potatoes are cut. They are fried in oil. They may be seasoned with salt. Some people add onion or garlic powder.

Restaurants often cook the potatoes twice. They start at a lower temperature. Then they turn up the heat. This makes the outsides crisp and golden. Yum!

A machine washes potatoes.

Many people buy frozen fries to cook at home. These are produced in a factory. The potatoes are placed on rollers. Dirt and eyes are removed. Next the potatoes are washed. Then they are sorted by size.

Machines steam the potato skins. This makes them soft. Next they are peeled and cut into strips. Then they are **blanched**. This protects the taste.

Finally, potatoes are fried and flash frozen. Packages are sent to restaurants and supermarkets. They just need to be reheated and enjoyed.

French fries move through a factory.

Potatoes are an excellent food choice. French fries are a tasty way to eat them. One potato makes about 25 french fries. And about one quarter of all potatoes in the U.S. end up as fries.

Eating fries too often isn't healthy. Peeling potatoes takes away healthy benefits. Frying adds fat. This can make foods less healthy. Baking fries in the oven is a better choice. This uses less oil. Some people use an **air fryer.**

Fries Around the World

Fast-food restaurants used to make their own fries. But in the 1950s, frozen fries were invented. This was great for business. Chains like McDonald's could open more restaurants. Back then an order of fries cost only 10 cents!

A menu shows McDonald's original prices.

HAMBURGER
CHEESEBURGER 15¢
FRENCH FRIES 19¢
MILK 10¢
10¢

ROOT BEER
ORANGEADE 10¢
COCA COLA 10¢
COFFEE 10¢

Today, McDonald's has millions of customers. They serve more fries than any other restaurant. They sell about 9 million pounds each day.

People in different countries like to eat their fries with different dips. Americans like ketchup. In the United Kingdom, fries are called chips. People sprinkle them with vinegar. Fish and chips is a traditional meal.

Mustard is used in France. People in Belgium eat fries with mayonnaise. Canadians have a dish called **poutine**. They cover fries with brown gravy and cheese curds.

You can also make fries with other vegetables. Many people love sweet potato fries. Or how about carrot fries? What's your favorite fry?

carrot, zucchini, and sweet potato fries

Make Your Own Oven Fries

Cooking fries in the oven is healthier than frying them. Try making your own crispy oven fries at home. Here's a healthy recipe to try with an adult.

What You Need:

- potatoes*
- cutting board
- sharp knife
- vegetable peeler
- large bowl
- paper towels
- baking sheet
- vegetable oil
- salt and pepper

*Russet potatoes are a good choice for making oven fries.

What You Do:

1. Preheat the oven to 375 degrees.

2. Have an adult help wash and peel the potatoes.

3. Ask an adult to cut the ends and sides off each potato to create a box shape. (This will make them easier to work with.) Then have an adult cut each potato into strips about 0.5 inch (0.13 centimeter) thick.

4. Soak the strips in cold water for 30 minutes. Then use a paper towel to pat them dry.

5. Place potatoes on a baking sheet. Lightly coat strips with vegetable oil. Then add salt and pepper to taste. (You can also use other seasonings such as garlic powder, onion salt, or dried herbs.)

6. Place baking sheet in the oven, and bake the potatoes for 10 minutes. Then turn up the temperature to 425 degrees. Bake for another 15-20 minutes or until crisp and golden.

7. Have an adult take the fries out of the oven. Enjoy eating!

*You can also make oven fries by leaving the skin on the potatoes.

Glossary

air fryer (AIR FRAHY-er)—a small, airtight appliance used for cooking food quickly using rapidly moving hot air

blanch (BLANCH)—to scald in order to remove the skin of something

nutrient (NOO-tree-uhnt)—parts of food, like vitamins, that are used for growth

poutine (poo-TEEN)—a dish of french fries covered in brown gravy and cheese curds

starch (STARCH)—a tasteless white carbohydrate that is an important part of rice, corn, wheat, beans, potatoes, and many other vegetables

White House (WAHYT HOUS)—the official Washington, D.C. home of the president of the United States

Read More

Mattern, Joanne. *French Fries*. Minneapolis: Bellwether Media, 2020.

Ransom, Candice. *French Fries*. Minneapolis: Cody Koala, an imprint of Pop!, 2019.

Stewart, Whitney. *What's On Your Plate?: Exploring the World of Food*. New York: Union Square Kids, 2023.

Internet Sites

BrightHub Education: The History of French Fries: Who Invented French Fries?
www.brighthubeducation.com/social-studies-help/123009-the-history-of-the-french-fry/

Kidadl: 27 Interesting Facts About French Fries You Should Know About!
kidadl.com/facts/27-interesting-facts-about-french-fries-you-should-know-about

Kiddle: French Fries Facts for Kids
kids.kiddle.co/French_fries

Index

About the Author

A public and a school librarian, Gloria Koster belongs to the Children's Book Committee of Bank Street College of Education. She enjoys both city and country life, dividing her time between Manhattan and the small town of Pound Ridge, New York. Gloria has three adult children and a bunch of energetic grandkids.